I Got a Pet!

My Pet Hamster

By Brienna Rossiter

www.littlebluehousebooks.com

Little Blue House is distributed by North Star Editions:
sales@northstareditions.com | 888-417-0195

Produced for Little Blue House by Red Line Editorial.

Photographs ©: Shutterstock Images, cover, 4, 7, 9, 10–11, 12, 15, 16–17, 20 (top), 20 (bottom), 24 (top left), 24 (top right), 24 (bottom left), 24 (bottom right); iStockphoto, 19, 23

Library of Congress Control Number: 2022901951

ISBN
978-1-64619-590-9 (hardcover)
978-1-64619-617-3 (paperback)
978-1-64619-669-2 (ebook pdf)
978-1-64619-644-9 (hosted ebook)

Printed in the United States of America
Mankato, MN
082022

About the Author

Brienna Rossiter is a writer and editor who lives in Minnesota.

Table of Contents

My Pet Hamster

I have a hamster.

It is small and soft.

My hamster lives in a cage.

I keep the cage on a table in my room.

cage

The cage has shavings inside. My hamster digs in the shavings.

shavings

The cage has tubes.
My hamster runs through
the tubes.

tube

wheel

Playtime

I watch my hamster play in its cage.
The cage has a wheel.
My hamster runs in the wheel.

Sometimes I hold
my hamster.
It sits in my hands.

I give my hamster seeds and treats.
It holds them in its cheeks.

cheek

I put my hamster in a ball. Then I put the ball on the floor. My hamster runs. It makes the ball roll.

ball

food
water

Hamster Care

I take good care of my hamster.

I give my hamster food to eat.

I give it water to drink.

I keep my hamster's shavings clean. I also give it paper to chew.

paper

Glossary

shavings

tube

treats

wheel

Index